100 Questions and Answers About East Asian Cultures

Michigan State University
School of Journalism

Read The Spirit Books

an imprint of
David Crumm Media, LLC
Canton, Michigan

For more information and further discussion, visit
news.jrn.msu.edu/culturalcompetence

Cover art and design by
Rick Nease
www.RickNeaseArt.com

Published by
Read The Spirit Books
an imprint of
David Crumm Media, LLC
42015 Ford Rd., Suite 234
Canton, Michigan, USA

For information about customized editions, bulk purchases or
permissions, contact David Crumm Media, LLC at
info@DavidCrummMedia.com

Contents

Foreword

By Helen Zia

When I was a kid growing up in New Jersey, I was an "ABC"—American-born Chinese of immigrant parents. But it made no difference whether I was born in North Jersey or North China, Japan or Korea, Vietnam, the Philippines or anywhere else in Asia—because I was routinely asked the same questions whenever I met some Anglo-American. "What are you?" they would pointedly ask, in a common variation of the equally common, "Where are you from?" asked as though I couldn't possibly be from New Jersey. Astonishingly, many of my questioners would then attempt to answer their own question in the belief that they could tell what country I was from by looking at my face. (They never guessed the correct answer: America!)

Listening to one person after another struggle to name the few Asian countries they ever heard of taught me at an early age how little most Americans knew about Asia or Asian people and cultures. "Are you from Taiwan? I just love Thai food!" some would exclaim, confusing Thailand with Taiwan. For the most part, the questions were well-meaning, just ill-informed. How I wished for some easy material to hand my questioners, short of sending them back to school or the library.

Knowledge today may have improved from the days when I was a kid, but the gaps are still there. "100 Questions and Answers About East Asian Cultures" is exactly what is needed to cut through the fog of ignorance about the world's largest and most populous continent. It couldn't come at a better time, as Asia steps onto center stage in this 21st century and people from all over Asia come to America in increasing numbers —as visitors and immigrants, students and scholars, professionals and refugees. Now, finally, when someone tries to guess where I am from or "what I am," I can hand them "100 Questions and Answers About East Asian Cultures," after I answer that I am "from" New Jersey. It is a joy to read and a valuable tool to share.

Helen Zia, a journalist and scholar, has dedicated her career to covering Asian-American communities and social and political movements. She is a former executive editor of Ms. Magazine and the author of "Asian American Dreams: The Emergence of an American People." With Wen Ho Lee, she wrote "My Country Versus Me: The First-Hand Account by the Los Alamos Scientist Who Was Falsely Accused of Being a Spy."

Preface

By Jane Hyun

Changing demographics and a globally connected workplace have placed us on a path toward a multicultural society. Yet, even with the best of intentions for understanding someone from a different culture, we lack reliable information for starting the dialogue.

Trust and respect are foundational to all healthy relationships, but what do you do when the practices of multicultural communities around you are at odds with how you would do things? Popular media may add to the confusion as too often, because of the lack of information, there is a tendency to rely on stereotypes and we are left with little distinction between fact and caricature.

Kudos to the students and faculty at Michigan State for this great feat. They have compiled an easy-to-read guide for understanding basic facts and cultural customs about East Asians. This resource provides important information that will dispel stereotypes, provide historical context where appropriate, and challenge you to investigate further for deeper understanding.

After reading this book, readers may decide to gain a greater cultural self-awareness and take steps to develop a better dialogue with their fellow students, colleagues and neighbors. Getting to know someone of a different culture is done one relationship at a time and there is richness that will come out of increased cross-cultural exchange.

I look forward to seeing how we engage the next level of conversation.

Jane Hyun is a leadership consultant and coach, and Author of "Flex: The New Playbook for Managing Across Differences" (2014) and "Breaking the Bamboo Ceiling: Career Strategies for Asians" (2005).

About the Series

This series of guides to cultural competence is designed to use journalistic tools to replace bias and stereotype with information. Guides are published by the Michigan State University School of Journalism. We create guides that are factual, clear and accessible.

We begin these guides by asking people to tell us the questions that people ask about them and others in their group. Some of the questions are simple. The answers almost never are, and one size does not fit all.

Sometimes, we must interpret the questions or look for the meaning behind them. Our goal is to answer the first-level questions in ways that are accurate, authoritative and accessible. So, we search for answers in studies, surveys and research. We ask experts.

These guides are intended to be just the first step to more conversations and greater understanding.

About this Guide

Asia is vast.

It is the largest continent on Earth in both geography and population. More than 4 billion of the world's people—over 60 percent—live in Asia.

Asian cultures are rich in diversity with varied languages, religions and customs.

This guide focuses on people from part of Asia, the region including China, Taiwan, Macau, Hong Kong, Japan, South and North Korea and Mongolia. This region is the place of origin for many people visiting in the United States and many who immigrate to the United States and become citizens. Another guide in this series focuses on South Asia, especially India.

Our focus here is not on Asian Americans, but on Asians studying or working in the United States. The 2013 International Institute for Education's Open Doors report indicates that more than 42 percent of all international students in the United States in 2012-2013 came from China, Taiwan, South Korea and Japan.

The questions posed within this guide are drawn from interviews with East Asians who said these are topics that Americans frequently ask them about or should know about. Using an array of research techniques, American and Asian students helped answer the questions. This guide to cultural competence addresses everyday questions and assumptions, and provides responses, perspective and context. The guide was developed to help Americans navigate cultural uncertainty when they engage with East Asians within the United States. If visiting an East Asian country, expectations would be different and a greater degree of cross-cultural understanding and behavior would be warranted.

Our goal was to be concise and clear, although cultural understanding is rarely simple. There is usually a lot behind each question. We hope these 100 questions and responses challenge you to learn more about East Asian cultures. By doing so, it is very possible you will better understand your own culture. There are resources at the end, but the best way to learn more about other people is to have conversations with them. Talk to lots of people because no two are the same.

Thank you.

Dawn Thorndike Pysarchik & Joe Grimm
Guide editors

Joe Grimm
Series editor
Michigan State University
College of Communication Arts and Sciences

Acknowledgments

Students who worked on this guide were members of a class in international advertising in the Michigan State University Department of Advertising and Public Relations. The team includes students who are American, Asian-American, Chinese, Taiwanese, South Korean and Japanese. The authors are: Aleena Bobich, HwiYeon Choi, Rachel Countegan, Michelle Cusick, Hannah Engwall, JiaJi Feng, Carly Hill, Jared McCarthy, Jun Peng, Melissa Poskey, Samuel Riddle, Lauren Semrau, Taesup Shin, Leah Socia, Zhenqi Tan, Zih-Han Tang, Alicia Vignoe, Rachel Wildt, Ruina Zhao and Xu Zhao.

Experts in several areas patiently gave advice or helped on the guide and we thank them for making it so much better. They include:

* Ken Moritsugu, Japan bureau chief, Associated Press
* Xiao Zhang, senior researcher, CLSA, Beijing
* Fu Zhibin, deputy editor-in-chief, China Today

* Roland Hwang, attorney, Michigan Department of Attorney General
* Tai Chan, environmental health and safety professional; president of Acacia168, LLC
* Amy Wu, university lecturer, Hong Kong Shue Yan University
* Soojung Chang, formerly speechwriter and researcher for The Permanent Mission of the Republic of Korea to the United Nations
* Akiko Matsuda, reporter, The Journal News
* Evelyn Hsu, senior director, programs and operations, the Maynard Institute for Journalism Education
* Liu Jian, reporter/editor, ChinAfrica, Beijing Review, China International Publishing Group
* Geri Alumit Zeldes, associate professor, Michigan State University School of Journalism
* Paulette Granberry-Russell, senior advisor to the president for diversity; director, Office for Inclusion and Intercultural Initiatives, Michigan State University
* Jessica Garcia, associate director, faculty and instructional development, Michigan State University
* Hui Hua Chua, collections and user support librarian, Michigan State University Libraries
* Nichole Igwe, independent study student, Michigan State University

Introduction

By Sook Wilkinson

When I was a graduate student in 1972 at Peabody in Nashville, Tenn., there weren't many Asian students. Most conversations started with, "Are you Chinese?" Upon hearing, "No, I'm from Korea," the next question usually was either, "North or South?" or, "Where's Korea?" Now, things have changed, and Asians are the fastest growing group of all immigrants in the United States. Our friends and colleagues are more and more informed about Asian Americans and their countries of origin.

Having a degree from an American university has opened up many doors for international graduates. It certainly was my dream, and one shared by many in Asian countries. Therefore it is not surprising that 49 percent of the international students in the United States now come from China, India or South Korea. These students and their families build bridges to far-off countries and often bring global perspectives and innovative ideas. We want to extend our heartfelt welcome to them.

This book of "100 Questions and Answers about East Asian Cultures" is a conversation starter. It can serve as a quick guide to making contact with and understanding international students and immigrants from Asian countries.

Sook Wilkinson is author of "Birth is More than Once: The Inner World of Adopted Korean Children," co-editor of "After the Morning Calm: Reflections of Korean Adoptees" and co-editor of a book about the experiences of Asian Americans in Michigan and the Midwest to be published in 2015. She is the board vice-chair at Northern Michigan University, and a board member of Asian & Pacific Islander American Health Forum.

Geography & Politics

1 What is East Asia?

The region is defined in various ways by geography, language and culture. This guide focuses on places that the United Nations Population Division designates as Eastern Asia. This includes the People's Republic of China and two special administrative regions—Hong Kong and Macau— Taiwan, Japan, South and North Korea and Mongolia. Some questions in this guide can be applied to other Asians in nearby regions, so some answers could also apply.

2 Why is East Asia's population so large?

China is the world's largest country by population, with almost 20 percent of the world's population, according to the U.S. Census Bureau. It is also the world's second largest country for land area, after Russia, according to the World Factbook. Two of the most densely crowded places in the world are special administrative regions of China: Macau (No. 1 with 52,000 people per square mile) and Hong Kong (No. 4 with 16,900 people per square mile). With about 83 people per square mile, the Chinese mainland has four times as many people per square mile as the United States. One of the world's least crowded countries, Mongolia, with just five people per square mile, is also in East Asia.

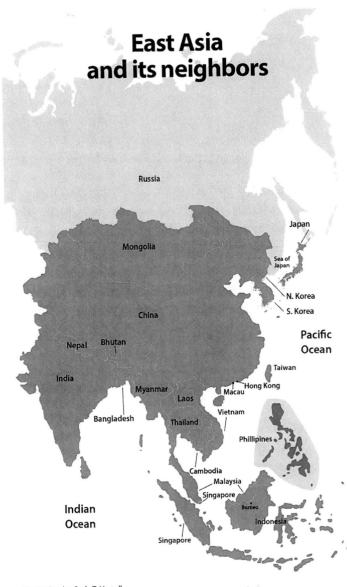

East Asia
and its neighbors

Russia

Mongolia

Japan

Sea of
Japan

N. Korea

S. Korea

China

Pacific
Ocean

Nepal   Bhutan

India

Taiwan

Myanmar   Hong Kong
           Macau

Laos

Bangladesh

Vietnam

Thailand

Phillipines

Cambodia

Malaysia

Singapore

Indian
Ocean

Borneo

Indonesia

Singapore

illustration by Cody T. Harrell

(Inner Mongolia is one of five autonomous regions in China.) East Asia has some of the oldest civilizations in the world. Other than Mongolia, East Asian countries have a generally habitable climate, good growing conditions and access to water.

3 What are major differences between East and Southeast Asia?

The difference is mainly geographic, but there are also some cultural, political and language differences. Major countries in Southeast Asia, according to the United Nations designation, include Vietnam, Cambodia, Thailand, Indonesia, Laos, Malaysia, Myanmar, the Philippines and Singapore. These have distinct languages, cultures and religions, and variations within each country.

4 Is there animosity among East Asian countries?

There have been books written about the multiple conflicts throughout the region, which are largely due to expansionism. While conflicts in the region have been ongoing for centuries, in 1894-1895 and 1937-1945, Japan was the aggressor against China in two wars, along with other confrontations. Japan sought to expand its empire and seize the Korean Peninsula, the Chinese mainland and Taiwan. More recently, wars in Korea and Vietnam have involved several nations in the region. Mistrust and tensions persist.

5 What are the disputes about the East Sea and the South China Sea?

The major focus is about territory and access to oil and gas reserves. South Korea and Japan are in a dispute over control of the Sea of Japan, which the South Koreans call the East Sea. The South China Sea is the focus of a territorial dispute between China and the Philippines. Both seas are part of the Pacific Ocean.

6 Where in the United States do the most people of East Asian descent live? Why?

The U.S. Census Bureau reports that more than 40 percent of all Asian Americans have East Asian ancestry. Most settle in California and along the West Coast. Early American laws that restricted Asian immigrants to certain areas in cities created communities that attracted others. There is a secondary concentration on the East Coast of the United States. Relocation programs of Asian refugees by the U.S. State Department created additional pockets in various states. Flights from the coasts provide faster connections to Asia, which are essential for family and business.

7 Is it OK to ask Asians, "Where are you from?"

Do this with care. The question can imply that the person does not belong here. This can offend Asian Americans, millions of whom were born here and whose families have been in the United States for generations. Second, people may ask about places of origin to try to learn about race or nationality. Then, answers such as, "I am from Seattle" might lead to other questions that can be offensive. "No, where are you REALLY from?" or "No, before that?" Some people do not wish to have their identities boiled down to labels. Get to know the individual as a person. Other answers will emerge.

8 What is the difference between South Korea and North Korea?

Korea was one country that came under the rule of the Empire of Japan from 1910 until the end of World War II. After the surrender of Japan, allied forces divided Korea. The United States occupied the southern half and Soviet forces occupied the sector north of the 38th parallel. Divisions deepened and the country divided in the early 1950s. Today, North Korea, the People's Democratic Republic of Korea, is a dictatorship. South Korea, the Republic of Korea, became a Western-style democracy. According to Human Rights Watch, North Korea criminalizes people who leave the country without permission, and it is hard to get permission. It is unnecessary and can be awkward to ask Koreans in the United States which Korea they are from.

9 Do Hmong people live in East Asia?

Long ago, the Hmong lived in southern China, but moved to the hill and mountain areas in Southeast Asia. They are ethnically Chinese. They have maintained their customs and language while living in Myanmar, Laos, Thailand and Vietnam. Most Hmong in the United States emigrated after the Vietnam War. The American CIA recruited the Hmong to oppose the Viet Cong in what has been called the "Secret War." After the United States pulled out of the war in 1975, the Hmong were persecuted for their involvement and many fled to Thailand. In the late 1980s, many were brought to the United States as refugees and sponsored by the Lutheran Church. The largest concentrations are in St. Paul, Minn., and Fresno, Calif., where the government set up resettlement areas.

Government

10 What type of governments do East Asian countries have?

People in the region live under one of the widest spectrums of governments in the world, from dictatorial to democratic. According to The World Factbook 2013-2014:

- People's Republic of China: communist state in which leaders are chosen from the Chinese Communist Party
- Taiwan: multiparty democracy with an elected legislature, a president and a premier. China describes Taiwan as "China's Taiwan" or "the Taiwan Region," reflecting their disagreement over its status.
- Japan: constitutional monarchy with an elected legislature that chooses the prime minister
- South Korea: constitutional democracy in which a constitution spells out the sovereign power of the people
- North Korea: hereditary dictatorship in which the ruler holds absolute power
- Mongolia: parliamentary government in which an elected legislature selects the government

11 What is the difference between China and Taiwan?

China, known as the People's Republic of China, is on the mainland. Taiwan, known as the Republic of China, is a large island off the coast. The capital city of China is Beijing, and the capital city of Taiwan is Taipei. The split began in 1895 when Japan seized the island of Taiwan. After World War II, Taiwan came under Chinese Nationalist control. Following the communist victory on the mainland, nationalists fled to Taiwan and set up a new government. The two governments have been at odds ever since. Mainland China treats Taiwan as a province and the United Nations does not recognize Taiwan as a country. This remains a highly sensitive topic. It is a significant matter whether a person identifies as Chinese or Taiwanese.

12 Is Hong Kong different from China?

Hong Kong is a special administrative region in southern China. This former British colony was handed over to the Chinese mainland in 1997. Hong Kong has a high degree of autonomy from the People's Republic of China in political and economic matters but not in foreign and defense affairs. Hong Kong was colonized by Britain from 1841 to 1997, and occupied by Japan from 1941 to 1945, when it was surrendered to the British. With more than 7 million people, Hong Kong is a densely populated financial center with a strong currency and many international visitors. Many would suggest that the culture, while similar to mainland China's, is different.

13 Do East Asian governments oppress people?

The range of freedom in East Asia is as wide as its array of governments. According to Amnesty International and Freedom House, Japan, South Korea, Mongolia and Taiwan value freedom. The organizations said political arrests, imprisonment, and censorship keep the People's Republic of China low on the list. They reported that the most oppressive regime in East Asia is North Korea.

14 What do the Japanese think about the United States and World War II?

In August 1945, the United States dropped atomic bombs on the cities of Hiroshima and Nagasaki, Japan. More than 200,000 died. These bombings ended the conflicts of World War II, and eventually led to the San Francisco Peace Treaty between the two countries in 1952. Following the treaty, the two countries began to trade with one another and became military allies in the 1960s. Despite trade friction in the 1990s, Japan and America are strong economic, political and military allies. According to a 2013 Pew Research Center poll, 69 percent of Japanese have a favorable view of the United States.

Values

15 Does a single culture dominate East Asia?

Like other continents or regions such as the Americas, Europe or Africa, East Asia has many cultures. For example, China recognizes 56 ethnicities and has many subcultures. People from one country can be offended if assumed to be from another, given their painful historical conflicts. Even within one country, people have regional and geographic differences, just like in the United States. East Asians do, however, share some basic values such as Confucianism, respect for elders and education.

16 Do Asians value group success more than individual success?

Generally, yes. This can be seen as the difference between emphasizing "I" or "we." It is the degree to which culture is individualist or collectivist. Many East Asian cultures are based on Confucian ideology, which teaches ethics and values, and the importance of community over individuality. In collective "we" cultures, people operate to advance the in-group, including family. They rely on the group for support and are loyal to it. Individualism reflects the value of self-reliance. One takes care of close family members, but does not generally depend on groups. According to rankings by the Hofstede Centre of Culture and

Management, the United States is the most individualistic society in the world. Asian and South American societies are generally toward the collective end of the scale.

17 Is this collective orientation related to "family honor" in Asian culture?

Traditionally, the extended family is of central value and lived under one roof. Members can have predetermined roles and obligations. Because education is viewed as an investment in the well-being of the family, this implies that the education of a family member is the responsibility of all. Education reflects positively on the family, yet can create expectations and pressure for offspring to succeed.

18 What does "save face" or "lose face" mean in East Asia?

Think of this as public humiliation for loss of reputation or stature. One can lose face when publicly corrected or confronted, especially by a peer or subordinate. One gains respect when bolstered or affirmed. With origins in China, this is more keenly a part of East Asian tradition than that of America. When the need to save face is strong, it can be difficult to openly admit mistakes or discuss problems. Even in one-to-one conversations and negotiations, people can feel the need to save face. When confronted with a situation of this nature involving an East Asian, consider feelings and not just the facts.

19 Why do some East Asians apologize so often?

When Asians say "sorry," it may not be an apology. Sometimes, "sorry" means, "excuse me," or "pardon me." If someone steps in front of you and says "sorry," they are just saying, "excuse me." This is another manifestation of humility, which is an important part of Asian cultures.

20 What is the value of humility or modesty?

Rooted thousands of years ago in Confucianism in China, this value is shared across East Asia. There are many aspects to Confucianism, but generally it holds that it is most respectful to not call attention to oneself and boast of one's merits. If you are boastful, you are behaving as the "village idiot rather than a scholar," according to Confucian teachings. Some people learn to accept compliments with a "thank you," but public praise can still feel uncomfortable.

Customs

21 Are there different Asian customs for bowing?

Bowing is both a traditional greeting and a gesture of respect. Modern Chinese society has de-emphasized bowing, while Japan and Korea continue the practice. Bows can express apology, gratitude, respect to elders and more. Different regions have different traditions with nuanced meanings. Bows range from informal to very formal. Informal bows are made at roughly 15-degree angles, while formal bows are made at 30 degrees. Very formal bows, not very common today, are usually deeper, at 90 degrees. In certain cases, such as a situation where great respect is being expressed, a kneeling bow will be performed. A kneeling bow, called kowtow in Cantonese, is to kneel and then bow so deeply that one's forehead touches the floor.

22 How should an American greet an East Asian person?

When in the United States, there is no need to greet an Asian person in a special way. Asians are generally not expecting an American to greet them in their own language or tradition. A simple smile, a "hello," or a handshake is sufficient. Also, as Asian countries all have different languages and traditions, it is tricky to greet an Asian in a culturally correct way. Saying "Konnichiwa," which is

Japanese, to people of a different Asian nationality would be inappropriate. Stick with what you know and act as you would with anyone.

23 Are there different gift-giving traditions in East Asia?

Although each Asian culture is different, gift giving is usually appropriate and expected during special occasions such as the New Year, birthdays, a new job or a first business meeting. Gifts don't have to be expensive, but they should be appropriately wrapped. The act of giving matters as much as the gift. You should not give clocks to Chinese friends, as the word for clock in Chinese sounds like "I will attend your funeral." A gift that has a set of four items is also considered unlucky in several East Asian cultures. Traditionally, East Asians don't open gifts right away. So, if someone sets your gift aside, it does not mean he or she doesn't like it; it is just a way of receiving gifts. This practice, too, is changing.

24 Are East Asians generally more reserved than Americans?

This can be true for reasons of culture and comfort. First, quietness and silence, for some, is a virtue in many Asian cultures. This can be traced to the Buddhist ideal of maintaining a passive and peaceful life. Secondly, many Asians in America are in a completely new cultural environment. Anyone might find English to be overwhelming at first. It can be difficult to interpret a certain American idiom or respond to a joke. American humor is not like that of other cultures. However, some Asians are the opposite of reserved and quiet and will fit right in when comfortable with another culture.

25 Are East Asians reluctant to mix with others in a foreign country?

The short answer is no. One reason people leave their country to study or work in a foreign country is to meet and experience new cultures. However, when encountering a culture that is so different from their own, such as in the United States, people still like to be with people who share their language and cultural identity. This does not mean they are reluctant to mix. International guests often speak of wanting to make new friends but don't know how to make American friends. Make the first move. Ask to join them or invite them to casual situations, such as coffee or an event, and plan on more meetings.

26 Why do some Asians walk so close together or hold hands when walking?

People from several cultures like to walk close together and hold hands or link arms with companions. This is neither confined to Asian cultures nor practiced by all Asian cultures. This is merely a way to express friendship.

27 Why do some Asians take on an "American" name when they come to America, and do they prefer the new name?

This is a personal choice and it is more prevalent among Chinese than others. Many people use their original names to show family respect. Others may change their names or add an American name to be called. This can be because their Asian names are hard to pronounce in English or to help Americans remember their name. It is not advisable to ask Asians for their "other" (original) name. Use the name they give you. If they give you two, ask which they prefer to be called.

28 Why is everyone named Lee or Kim?

Although these are popular names, not everyone from East Asia is named Lee or Kim (or variations like Rhee or Gim). The names are not exclusive to Asia, either. Lee is one of the most popular surnames in Britain. As in the United States, there are many last names and some occur more than others. Lee and Li are popular Korean and Chinese names; Kim is a popular Korean surname. However, do not assume a nationality from a name, any more than someone should assume that everyone with your last name must live in your state and that you all know each other.

29 What is feng shui?

Feng shui originated in China thousands of years ago. It means "wind-water." It is focused on creating good energy, which brings good fortune. Feng shui can have different underlying dimensions that can impact the orientation, architecture and environment of a building. It can mean clearing out clutter and positioning objects like aquariums, crystals and fountains, which welcome prosperity and good fortune.

Traditions

30 Why do Chinese wear white or black at funerals but red at weddings?

White, black and dark blue are traditional colors at Chinese funerals, but red and gold are celebratory colors for weddings. Because of its association with death, white is typically not worn at a traditional Chinese wedding. In modern Chinese weddings, the bride might change dresses, wearing both a white wedding gown and a traditional red bridal dress.

31 There's Japanese kendo and judo, Korean taekwondo, and Chinese kung fu and tai chi. Does Asian culture encourage fighting?

Many of these martial arts don't focus just on fighting. They came about as forms of self-defense, self-control and fitness, rather than for attack. Kendo is a traditional Japanese style of fencing that strives to coordinate physical, emotional and mental dimensions. Judo actually translates to "the gentle way." It stresses defense by using opponents' offensive energy against them. Taekwondo works on control of one's mind, self-restraint, kindness and humility. Kung fu describes an individual accomplishment reached after hard work, which is strongly linked to Buddhism through humility and restraint. Tai chi works on the concept of yin-yang, or duality and balance. It is mainly a meditative exercise rather than a fighting form.

32 What are major holidays for East Asians?

While celebratory customs differ, most of these countries have a New Year's Day, a National Day, and a Children's Day. Some have days dedicated to ancestors or the elderly. When traveling to an East Asian country, find out the dates of the holidays. Many are set to the lunar calendar, which is different every year, and you might find that public and business offices will be closed. There are some differences among countries, and not all countries use the lunar calendar.

- In China, the most important holiday is the Chinese New Year, or Spring Festival. It can last about a week and is a time for visiting families, especially if travel is required. New Year's, the Qingming Festival for ancestors, the summer Dragon Boat Festival, and the Mid-Autumn Festival are statutory public holidays.

- Korea has Buddha's Day in April or May, depending on the lunar calendar. There's also Chuseok, the biggest holiday of the year, when there is a harvest moon. It is often referred to as Korean Thanksgiving. Sul Nal is the Korean New Year's day on the lunar calendar. Parents' Day, Children's Day, Teachers' Day, Constitution Day and National Foundation Day are other Korean holidays.

- In Japan, people celebrate New Year's on Jan. 1, not according to the lunar calendar, and the emperor's birthday is a national holiday. Japan also celebrates the Doll's Festival (also known as Girls' Festival),

Obon to commemorate ancestors, and Children's Day (formerly known as Boys' Festival).

33 How do Asians celebrate the Lunar New Year?

Lunar New Year is a huge family reunion. Traditionally, people in China wear red or brightly colored clothes. Children and unmarried people receive "lucky money" in red envelopes. The red symbolizes fire and drives away bad luck. In fact, people in China used to light bamboo stalks because the crackling flames would frighten evil spirits. Fireworks are associated with the Lunar New Year, as are lanterns decorated with art, birds, animals, flowers and zodiac signs. A dance with a long dragon made of bamboo, silk, and paper that snakes through the streets is traditional in China. In Korea, people wear their traditional dress "hanbok," eat special foods and play special games.

34 What is the meaning of different animal years and the Chinese Zodiac?

According to Chinese legend, Buddha asked all animals to meet him on the Lunar New Year. Twelve animals came, so Buddha named a year after each one. People born in each animal's year would have some of that animal's characteristics, both desirable and undesirable. The Zodiac animals are rat, ox, tiger, rabbit, dragon, snake, horse, sheep, monkey, rooster, dog and pig. Chinese people don't all take this seriously.

35 Are there different beliefs associated with specific numbers in East Asia?

There are many. Some believe that the number two suggests harmony, while the number three indicates multiples and, in Buddhist culture, represents Buddha, Dharma and Bonze. Four is considered unlucky, similar to how some Western cultures think that the number 13 is unlucky. The Mandarin, Cantonese, Korean and Japanese words for "four" sound like the word for "death." Six in Chinese is pronounced as "Liu," which sounds like the word for "doing everything smoothly." Seven implies holiness and mystery in Buddhism, as well as luck. The number eight is considered auspicious because eight is pronounced "Ba" in Chinese. This sounds similar to the Chinese word "Fa," which means to make a fortune. In the 1990s, a license plate with the number eight was auctioned for 5 million Hong Kong dollars. The number nine in Japanese sounds like "Ku," which connotes suffering, while nine in Chinese means longevity and 10 implies completeness.

Pop Culture

36 What are manga and anime?

Manga, a type of comic, developed in Japan. Manga have evolved stylistically and have become popular around the world. With roots in manga and Western cartoons, anime is a style of animation that was started by manga artist Osamu Tezuka after World War II. Tezuka was inspired by pre-war Disney cartoons and the character Betty Boop. Today, many manga have big heads and large expressive eyes. With their complex story lines and some adult content, manga have a broad appeal that ranges among children and adults.

37 What is Hello Kitty and what is "kawaii?"

Hello Kitty is a group of characters revolving around a white cat, just five apples tall, named Kitty White, or Kitty-chan. Japanese designer Yuko Yamaguchi created Hello Kitty in 1974 and made Kitty-chan British because England was a trendy place for Japanese culture at the time. Hello Kitty has long since expanded beyond the young adult market and has appeared in animations and on guitars, computers and wine. There are even Hello Kitty weddings and jets. Hello Kitty has a certain kawaii, which is Japan's pop-culture quality of cuteness.

38 Why are East Asians so obsessed with idols?

Sports idols are celebrated in East Asia just as they are in the United States. Fame and celebrity also help export pop culture, goodwill—and merchandise. In South Korea, the country with East Asia's youngest average age, K-pop—Korean music—reigns. This visual, danceable fusion of popular music styles created numerous celebrities and groups. The appeal of K-pop artists is in their fashion sense, dance moves and catchy songs. Social media such as YouTube carry K-pop around the world. Similarly, J-pop—Japanese pop— music was born in the 1990s. It has gained popularity and its artists have influenced the music scene throughout Asia.

39 What is "hallyu" or the Korean wave?

Korean entertainment and pop culture has become a top export of Korea. It's happening with pop music, TV dramas and movies. It's called the Korean wave in many countries, and hallyu in Korean. It began with the release of the movie "Oldboy" in 2003, which gained international acclaim. K-pop stars have fans around the world. Examples include Girls' Generation, a nine-member South Korean girl group, and Psy, the Korean rapper and songwriter known for having more than 1.9 billion views on YouTube with his "Gangnam Style" video.

40 Did karaoke begin in Asia?

Karaoke originated in Japan in the 1970s and means "empty orchestra." In karaoke bars, patrons sing along to recordings of the instrumental parts of popular songs. Karaoke has become a popular way to socialize and relax in other Asian countries, as well. Karaoke came to the United States in the 1990s.

41 How are Asians portrayed in American movies and television?

According to the Media Action Network for Asian Americans, movies and television in the United States often show Asians in stereotypical ways, which is upsetting to many Asians and Asian Americans. Those include portraying Asians as outsiders or limited to certain occupations. Asian men are often portrayed as villains or emasculated as sexless nerds. Women are shown as sexy, subservient, conniving backstabbers or instantly charmed by white men. In the film industry, Asian actors and actresses have had trouble getting roles, even for Asian characters.

42 Do Asians like American culture and want to be part of it?

This varies from country to country and person to person. Feelings can be influenced by politics, economics and confidence in the home country's culture. The favorability of American culture in East Asia is declining. A 2012 Pew study found that 69 percent of Japanese said they liked American movies and television. This was down from 2002, but still in the top of the 20 countries surveyed. China, at 43 percent and dropping, was at the top of the lower third. A 2004 Rand report of South Koreans called "Ambivalent Allies" said, "the more secure they are about Korean culture, the less favorable their opinions are toward the United States."

Families

43 Why is family ancestry so important?

Ancestry is important not only to Asians but to many other societies in the world. Family lineage reflects where the family originated from, which is relevant to social status. Traditionally, it served as one of the few ways to determine whether a person was educated or noble. Family lineage meets people's needs for a sense of belonging.

44 What is behind the emphasis on respect for elders?

Many other parts of the world share this value. In East Asia, Confucianism encourages filial piety. This philosophy teaches people to acknowledge the care they received as children and to respect the elders and their ancestors. Respect often carries over to non-parental elders in social and business situations. There has been some concern that, with modernization, this value may be declining.

45 Do Asian parents try to control their children's lives?

Confucian principles of elder respect and collectivism intersect in parent-child interactions. Children are traditionally expected to defer big decisions to elders, and parents take a family interest in important issues such as education and marriage. The degree to which younger generations listen to their more experienced parents is variable and is affected by culture and personalities. This is changing, too.

46 What is China's "one-child policy?"

Beginning in 1979, this policy sought to control population growth by limiting couples to one child when one spouse was an only child. The policy allowed two children for couples who were both only children. There were exceptions for ethnic minorities and rural couples whose first child was a girl or disabled. The policy caused the birth rate to fall too far, the average age to rise and—coupled with social preferences for males, female abortion and infanticide—a gender imbalance. Recently, the policy was relaxed. Now, if one spouse is an only child the couple may have two children.

47 Why do some East Asians value males more than females?

This is not true of just East Asia. For centuries, patrilineal societies worldwide have favored male children to carry on the family name and lineage. In agrarian societies, males were more valued for agricultural work. Greater family status came to be tied to male children. These circumstances, of course, are changing all around the world.

48 Do East Asians get divorced and, if so, is it looked down upon?

Across East Asia, the divorce rate is rising. The UN's Department of Economic and Social Affairs reports a significant increase in divorce in East Asia. In 1970, the divorce rate in East Asian countries was less than one per 1,000 in population. By 2005, that had nearly tripled with the largest increases in Taiwan and South Korea. In 2011, the Korea Herald reported that the 2010 Korean census had shown a 40.2 percent increase in the number of divorced South Koreans since 2005. ChinaDaily.com reported that, "One of the less desirable ways in which China has followed the West is in the explosive growth of the divorce rate, which in the major cities is now approaching 40 percent of those married. All over the country, one encounters couples who have struggled together through the hard times and are still together, contentedly if not always happily, after 50 years, while their children's marriages have barely lasted 10 years."

49 Is it frowned upon to marry someone of another racial or ethnic group?

There were mixed marriages in East Asia even before the United States existed, but it has been controversial. Now, these marriages are increasing. According to the Chinese Ministry of Civil Affairs, the number of marriages between Chinese and foreign nationals, including Hong Kong, Taiwan and Macau, increased from about 11,000 couples in 1980 to 53,000 couples in 2012. Japan's Ministry of Health, Labour and Welfare reported that one in 20 marriages in 2003 were mixed. About 80 percent of the time, the husband was Japanese and the non-Japanese spouse was frequently Chinese, Korean, Filipino or American. Most of South Korea's mixed marriages are a Korean man marrying a non-Korean woman.

Language

50 If a person knows one East Asian language, is it easier to learn another?

Not really. Many of the languages have influenced each other, but they are not related linguistically and belong to different language families. Japanese and Korean use Chinese characters. That is where many of the similarities end. While some grammar patterns are similar, the languages sound very different. Chinese is a tonal language, whereas Japanese has little inflection.

51 What are the major spoken languages in China?

Standard spoken Chinese is Mandarin. It is the most-spoken language in the world with more speakers than Spanish and English combined. Other languages and dialects are spoken across China, but generally Mandarin unites the country. Cantonese is spoken in Guangdong province and overseas communities and is an official language of Hong Kong (with English) and Macau. People disagree whether Cantonese is a language or a dialect.

52 Does Japan have multiple languages?

Japan has one language, Japanese, with different dialects. Depending on the region of Japan, words, pronunciation and sentence endings may be different. In Okinawa, the differentiation in language is enough where it could be considered a branch of Japanese, but the government considers it a dialect.

53 Do South Korea and North Korea use the same language?

The countries were one long before they were divided, so there is not a significant difference in language. Many of the differences are only minor ones such as spelling and sound variations. One major difference, however, comes from borrowing words. South Korea has incorporated some words from English. North Korea, being a more closed nation and not as influenced by outside cultures, tries to keep its language pure, but has borrowed from neighboring China.

54 To what extent do people in Asia learn English?

Just as many Americans learn Asian languages, many Asians learn English. Many countries in the world include English classes in their educational systems. Many East Asian families place a high importance on learning English, and English language studies are commonplace in Asian schools. The focus is usually on grammar, reading and writing. This means that, while many students have taken many years of English, they still need experience speaking it.

To be admitted to U.S. universities, students must take the Test of English as a Foreign Language (TOEFL).

55 Is it difficult for East Asians to learn English?

Success in learning a language depends on how similar the language is to your own and when you begin. Asian languages are in a different family than English. Therefore, different written characters, grammar patterns and spoken sounds cause difficulty. Several Asian languages use tones or pitches to distinguish among words, while English does not. Some Asian languages do not distinguish between the L sound and the R sound, but English does. Here's another way to think about East Asian difficulties learning English: The U.S. Foreign Service Institute says that the toughest major languages for English speakers to learn are Mandarin, Cantonese, Korean, Japanese and Arabic.

Communication

56 Some East Asians seem to speak loudly and some seem quiet. Why is that?

Volume can have more to do with individual personalities and the situation a person is in than with language or culture. Even within families, people speak at different volumes. Every continent, however, has some tonal languages in which pitch can change the meaning of a word. Some Asian languages have more tones than others. Cantonese, for example, is very tonal, which affects the volume. On the other hand, English is not tonal. Therefore, the volume or pitch difference you might detect could be due to the tonal characteristics of Asian languages. Additionally, you will see differences among those who are reserved and those who are outgoing. An individual's comfort level in a setting may also account for speaking volume.

57 Does speaking slowly to English-language learners help them?

Several factors need to be taken into consideration. Speaking too slowly, too loudly or in a different voice can make people feel as though they are being treated like children. We typically can absorb words faster than we can say them, even in our native language. So, don't assume that a person who speaks slowly has to be spoken to that way.

Speak at a normal pace and look for expressions or body language cues to determine if the receiver is understanding what you are saying.

58 Why are Asians often quiet in meetings or social settings?

Stemming from cultural values, Asians generally talk less than Westerners. Keep in mind though, sometimes language fluency may keep individuals from speaking. Most Asian countries are described as high-context cultures. This means that verbal communications tend to be more indirect and ambiguous, and much of the meaning and understanding of a message is reflected in nonverbal cues. Therefore, it is unnecessary to use excessive words to transmit the meaning of a message. Also, Confucian and some religious values revere silence. This is an important aspect of communication and it is necessary for internalization of the message. Silence has meaning in East Asian cultures and reflects humility and respect for others.

59 If people don't talk, how do I know what they are thinking?

Even when people don't speak, they can still be communicating with you. Pay attention in different ways. Watch nonverbal cues, such as facial expressions and body language, for context and meaning. If Asians don't agree with something, they likely will not say anything at the time but later may express their views indirectly or through a letter or email message. The United States is a low-context country, as are many other Western countries. This means that messages are not "coded" with cultural context. Therefore, more detailed verbal discussion and words are needed to ensure that the precise meaning and understanding are conveyed. Low-context messages rely on the words used and are explicit.

Appearance

60 What gives East Asian eyes their distinctive shape?

The shape of many Asians' eyes is distinctive because of the epicanthic fold. This fold of skin from the upper eyelid arches over the inner corner of the eye, resulting in a less pronounced upper eyelid crease. The degree of the fold varies. Eyesight is unaffected because light enters the eye through the pupil at the center of the eye. Some Africans, Europeans and Native Americans also have epicanthic folds.

61 Do all Asians have black hair and black pupils?

Most do, but not all. Black is the most common hair color on the planet and it is the dominant hair gene. Some Asians, however, have brown hair, the second-most-common color. People from some regions, such as parts of western China, have lighter hair and eyes. The pupil, at the center of the eye, is black for almost everyone, but the iris surrounding it is usually brown in Asians.

62 Why is plastic surgery so popular in Korea?

Several trends have contributed to its popularity. Modernization, acceptance of plastic surgery, affordable operations and the popularity of pop idols have all been cited as contributing to this trend. The most common operations are the double eyelid fold to make the eye look larger and rounder and surgery to make the nose taller. A 2009 Trend Monitor survey of women aged 19-49 in Seoul found that one in five said she had undergone plastic surgery. Many patients are recent high school graduates, which has led to a backlash and controversy about whether this is necessary and appropriate.

63 Can East Asians tell each other's nationality on sight?

The ability to recognize people of one's own race is called the cross-race effect. It is an imperfect guessing game. Nationality, which isn't the same as race, is even harder to guess. Cues like clothing and jewelry might help, but then there is the growing trend of globalization. It is better not to guess, even about people who look like you.

64 Are Asians genetically smaller than Americans?

According to "Society at a Glance 2009" by the Organisation for Economic Co-operation and Development, nutrition plays a larger role in height than genetics. Other factors cited are healthcare and standard of living. The report said that the height gap is closing as countries with shorter average heights are catching up to taller ones. The report said that the average height of Americans has stagnated and that the "star performer" in adult height gain was South Korea.

Education

65 Why do Asians come to America for college?

With the large populations of college-aged students in Asian countries, the competition to enter elite universities can be intense. Many students choose to study in the United States if they don't get into their preferred university in their home country. The United States has a very large capacity for students with 4,000 accredited institutions. Many American colleges and universities are known for being of exceptional quality. In the 2014 Times Higher Education university rankings by Thomson Reuters, U.S. universities had eight of the top 10 rankings in the world and 27 of the top 50. An American education has been compared to a "luxury item." The Institute for International Education reported that 819,644 international students studied in colleges in the United States in 2012-2013.

66 Do Asians need government permission to study abroad?

To study in the United States, students must be accepted into an approved Student and Exchange Visitor Program school. From there, students work with the U.S. Department of State for a student visa.

67 Are there pressures from a student's home government or families to study in the United States?

It is more a matter of financial support, as studying overseas can cost families a lot of money. Governments, both in the United States and overseas, are increasing their support. East Asia does not currently have enough openings in universities to meet demand.

68 Do Asians have to be exceptionally wealthy to afford college in the United States?

Typically, tuition and expenses for an international student can be several times the rate paid by in-state students. While limited, some scholarships are available for East Asian students to study in the United States. Average incomes in Asian countries tend to be lower than the U.S. average income. That means that international students usually come from wealthier families.

69 Do most East Asians go to college?

The Organisation for Economic Co-operation and Development reported these levels for post-secondary education among people aged 25-64 for 2011: Japan, 46 percent; the United States, 41 percent; South Korea, 40 percent. China has made education a priority and is rapidly increasing the number of students with high school and post-secondary educations.

70 Are math and science emphasized in Chinese schools?

According to "Going to School in East Asia," China decided in 2001 to focus on creating well-rounded students. The curriculum includes history, geography, the arts, math, physical education, Chinese, a foreign language, integrated sciences, research-oriented study and technology. National entrance examinations consist of Chinese, English and math. There is also an integrated science test for science major applicants, or an integrated social science test for liberal arts or social science major applicants.

71 Are Asians obsessed with grades?

Highly competitive examination systems in East Asia pressure students and families to do well on exams. According to the BBC in 2013, a Euromonitor survey found that per capita disposable income in China increased by 63.3 percent from 2007 to 2012, while consumer spending on education increased by almost 94 percent. The report said another study estimated that 70 percent of Korean household spending went for private education. Good grades usually mean placement in more prestigious schools and, therefore, a return on the family's investment.

72 What are classrooms like in East Asian schools?

The Asia Society Educational Organization describes schools in South Korea this way: High school begins about 8 a.m. with a morning break and a 50-minute lunch. Afternoon classes run from 1 p.m. to 4 or 4:30 p.m. when students clean the classroom. Students may go home for dinner or eat at school. Students return to the school library to study or attend private schools or tutoring sessions until between 10 p.m. and midnight. Teachers move from room to room, but students stay in one place. The routine for lower grades is generally less intense. Many East Asian schools emphasize memorization and testing, and have a similar emphasis on education, which is coined "education fever."

Work & Money

73 Are most East Asian students in the United States wealthy and do they drive expensive cars?

This is an over-generalization. Tuition for international students is high, so many do come from wealthy families. However, the Chinese Academy of Social Sciences stated that a third of Chinese students studying abroad in 2010 were from working-class families. Some wealthy students do drive expensive cars. Businessweek.com reported that high import taxes in home countries could make expensive cars seem like a bargain in the United States. In that article, the president of CNW Marketing Research estimated that Chinese students in U.S. high schools and colleges spent about $15.5 billion on vehicles in 2012-2013. That is more than triple what a comparable group of U.S. students spent.

74 Do Asians studying in the United States focus on medicine, engineering and business?

A high number of international students in general come to study in some of these areas. American universities offer strong programs, and many will return home to take over the family business. The Institute for International Education reported in 2013 that the top fields of study for international students were business, 21.8 percent; engineering, 18.8 percent; and math and computer science, 9.5 percent.

75 How wealthy are Asians in the United States generally?

According to the Census Bureau's 2012 annual report on income, Asian households in the United States had the highest median income, $68,636. Asian households earned at least $10,000 more than any other ethnic group in the United States. Median household wealth is also higher than for all American adults, $83,500 versus $68,529. There is a wide range behind the numbers.

76 What is the "model minority myth?"

This is the belief that a particular ethnic, racial or religious group achieves greater success than the general population. In the United States, this myth often refers to Asians. Concerns are that the myth implies that some people get ahead because of the group they are in, or that group members who do not succeed are inferior. It ignores the history and ongoing experiences of discrimination these groups face and masks socioeconomic diversity within these groups.

77 Do people from East Asia work long hours?

According to the Organisation for Economic Co-operation and Development, in 2012 the average American worked 6.8 hours each day, while South Koreans averaged 8.0 hours a day and Japanese averaged 6.6 hours a day. The global average was 6.7 hours a day. The United Nations World Tourism Council, which favors time off, reported in 2010 that the average American worker had 13 vacation days per year and the average in Japan and Korea was 25. A 2012 Pew report said, "Asian Americans have a pervasive belief in the rewards of hard work. Nearly 70 percent say people can get ahead if they are willing to work hard, a view shared by a somewhat smaller share of the American public as a whole (58 percent)." Pew reported that 93 percent of Asian Americans "describe members of their country of origin group as 'very hardworking'; just 57 percent say the same about Americans as a whole."

78 Why do so many Asians in the United States work at nail salons?

Different immigrant groups gravitate toward businesses where they can get jobs and be successful. These tend to be service businesses with low startup costs that do not require extensive certification and licensing, and where families can work together. In some industries, members of the same ethnic group become suppliers or help set people up in business. This happened in the nail business in the mid 1970s after the fall of Saigon. The National Asian Pacific American Women's Forum reports that 42 percent of nail technicians in the United States are Asian, with 39 percent being Vietnamese and 2 percent South Korean.

79 Do a lot of Asians run their own businesses in the United States?

According to a 2011 U.S. Census Bureau report, "the number of U.S. businesses owned by people of Asian origin increased 40.4 percent to 1.5 million between 2002 and 2007, increasing at more than twice the national rate." According to a June 2012 report by the Fiscal Policy Institute's Immigration Research Initiative, Koreans are in the top 10 nationalities for highest rates of small-business ownership in the United States.

Religion

80 Are East Asians free to practice the religion they want?

Japan and South Korea have religious freedom. The U.S. Council on Foreign Relations reports that China's constitution calls for religious freedom, but that not all religions are recognized. The leading religion in China is Buddhism, followed by Christianity, Islam, Hinduism and other religions. The U.S. Department of State says that the way laws in China are applied does not meet international human rights standards. North Korea does not have genuine religious freedom.

81 What religions do Chinese people practice?

While China is officially atheist, many practice Buddhism, Taoism, Christianity, Islam and ancestor worship. Buddhism is the largest organized religion in China. There are many gods in Chinese myths and people hold different beliefs regarding them.

82 How is religion practiced in Japan?

In Japan, religions can be combined when they complement each other and coexist harmoniously. For example, Shintoism, an early Japanese religion, and Buddhism, an

Indian religion, are the two main religions in Japan and many people practice both. The religions share some gods and values, and their shrines can be built next to each other. Other religions are also practiced.

83 Is Christianity the same in East Asia as in America?

Certainly the beliefs are the same, but there is a big difference in participation. About 75 percent of Americans say they are Christian. In most East Asian countries, Christians are less than 5 percent of the population, according to The World Factbook 2013-2014. The exception is South Korea, where about a third of the population is Protestant or Catholic. The National Chinese Christian Congress said in 2013 that Christianity was increasing in China, despite reports of persecution and a crackdown on house churches.

84 Are South and North Korea religiously similar?

No. Both countries were traditionally Buddhist and Confucianist, but the separation changed that. Some would say that Confucianism is not a religion but that its ideology and teachings influence daily life. Christians moved south and independent religious practices were discouraged in the north. In South Korea, Buddhism, Protestantism and Catholicism are the largest religions. More than a third of South Koreans do not affiliate with an organized religion. The church plays an important social function for Korean communities in the United States.

Health & Medicine

85 What is traditional Chinese medicine and does it work?

Traditional Chinese medicine is not a single treatment or therapy. It is many practices connected by shared concepts. Practices include herbal medicine, plants, diet, exercise, massage and techniques such as acupuncture. It has been effective in pain management, for the common cold and cough, and treating contusions and sprains. Traditional Chinese medicine has been used for thousands of years. In the United States, most states have laws to regulate Traditional and Complementary Medicine.

86 What is the life expectancy in Asia?

The World Factbook 2013-2014 gave these estimates for 2013. Japan was ranked first in the world with an average life expectancy for men and women of 82.7. South Korea, at 80.7 years, was 24th. China was 58th with an average life expectancy of 75.6 and Mongolia was 157th at 69. The United States was 37th with a life expectancy of 78.6 years.

87 What are the infant mortality rates in East Asia and the United States?

The World Factbook 2013-2014 gives these estimates of infant deaths per 1,000 live births in 2013:

- Mongolia: 34.8
- North Korea: 25.3
- China: 15.2
- United States: 5.9
- Taiwan: 4.6
- South Korea: 4.0
- Macau: 3.2
- Hong Kong: 2.9
- Japan: 2.2

88 How efficient are health-care systems in East Asia?

According to a 2013 Bloomberg ranking, the most efficient health-care system in the world was in Hong Kong, followed by Singapore and Japan. South Korea was eighth. Far down the list was China at 37 and the United States at 46. Mongolia was not included.

89 Do East Asians smoke a lot of cigarettes?

Some do, but there is significant variation. According to a 2009 study by the World Lung Foundation and the American Cancer Society, the highest number of cigarettes smoked per person occurred in Eastern Europe and Russia. South Korea came in eighth, with 1,958 cigarettes per person a year, and Japan with 1,841. China was 11th with 1,711. The United States was 34th with 1,028 cigarettes per person.

Food

90 Is Asian food spicy?

Asian food varies from country to country and within countries.

- Chinese cuisine features many foods with a strong taste. China's eight major cuisines are: Lu, Min, Su, Zhe, Hui, Yue, Chuan and Xiang. Lu is not spicy and usually consists of seafood, soup, or a variety of bowls. Min cuisine is not spicy and mixes sweetness, sourness and saltiness. Su and Zhe cuisine are sweet. Hui is known for being moderately spicy and usually salty. Chuan is the second spiciest cuisine and is known for using Sichuan peppers. Xiang cuisine is the spiciest of the eight cuisines.

- Korean meals often include a number of side dishes and kimchi, a fermented vegetable that is usually cabbage. The meal is based on rice, vegetables and meat. Variations have spread beyond their original regions within Korea.

- Japanese cooking is heavily influenced by China and Korea but is relatively lighter and milder. It relies more heavily on seafood and vegetables.

91 Is Chinese food in the United States like Chinese food in China?

There are similarities and differences. Although there are authentic Chinese restaurants in the United States, most cater to American palates. Chinese food is traditionally rich in spices and vegetables, while American Chinese dishes emphasize meat, salt and sugar.

92 Do Chinese eat General Tso chicken in China?

Most Chinese do not know of this dish until they visit America. General Tso chicken is an American dish, just like chop suey and fortune cookies. Chop suey was created by Chinese in the United States for Americans and is made with onions, celery, and chopped up meat. Fortune cookies were invented by the Japanese and are uncommon in China.

93 Do Japanese eat sushi every day?

No. Sushi is a food for special occasions, not everyday meals, and some Japanese do not eat it at all. Some people confuse sushi with sashimi. Sushi is vinegared rice with a variety of toppings. Sashimi is sliced raw meat, usually seafood. Also, some sushi rolls, such as California rolls and dragon rolls, are American creations.

94 Why do some Asians eat food like chicken feet?

In many places, people with limited access to food learned to cook parts of animals that might not normally be eaten in other cultures. Nothing is wasted. These foods become part of tradition and sentiment and might still be eaten even when other choices are available.

95 Why do Asians eat so much rice?

Most of the world's rice is grown in Asia and eaten there, where it has been a staple for thousands of years. The Irrigated Rice Research Consortium reports that rice consumption per person has declined in China as people have added meat, dairy, fruits and vegetables to their diets. Rice consumption, however, has been growing in sub-Saharan Africa and in the United States and Europe, where people are adding fiber.

96 Why do some Asians decline dairy products?

Many Asian adults have trouble digesting lactose, a sugar found in milk and other dairy products. It can give them cramps, bloating and nausea. While about two thirds of adults worldwide have a lactose intolerance, according to the National Institute of Health's U.S. National Laboratory of Medicine, more than 90 percent of East Asian adults have this condition.

97 Are chopsticks used throughout Asia?

Not necessarily. Chopsticks originated in China around 1200 B.C. when cooks used them to retrieve food from the bottom of pots. Chopsticks moved from stove to table and became popular in China, Japan, Korea and Vietnam. People in Indonesia, Thailand and India don't traditionally use chopsticks. Some Southeast Asian restaurants run by people who don't generally use chopsticks offer them to Americans who believe this will help them eat more authentically.

98 Do some Asians still eat dog meat?

Yes, though the practice seems to be declining. When food was scarce, people had to eat what was available and dog meat was adopted. World opinion, animal welfare activists, laws and increased pet ownership is discouraging the practice. Although some Asian countries banned the sale of dog meat, some are slow to enforce the statutes. China banished dog meat from menus during the 2008 Olympic Games in Beijing. In 2014, the Vietnamese government cracked down on the illegal importation of dogs. Protests about the killing of strays at the 2014 Winter Olympics in Sochi immediately put pressure on South Korea, which will host the 2018 Winter Olympics, to discourage this practice.

99 Is tea important in East Asia?

Tea is important and has different traditions in every East Asian country. China is the leading producer of the world's most popular beverage and has been drinking it for centuries. More than just a beverage, tea is used in medicines and food. China, Japan and Korea all have different traditions for preparing and serving tea. In Mongolia, tea is prepared with milk and salt and served with food such as noodles.

100 Do some East Asians drink a lot of alcohol?

Alcohol consumption worldwide varies considerably, accordingly to different reports. The World Health Organization reported in 2011 that South Korea was 12th in the world for per-capita alcohol consumption, the United States was 57th, Japan was 70th and China was 96th. Euromonitor reported in 2013 that South Korea was first in liquor consumption, with more than double the amount of second-place Russia. Many Asians avoid alcohol because of "Asian flush," a reaction to alcohol that causes the skin to flush with red blotches. The Chinese do a lot of toasting at business dinners with wine or strong liqueurs.

Resources

Adachi, Nobuko. *East Asian Transnational Migrants and Culture in a Global World*. Abu Dhabi, UAE: Zayed University Press, 2012. Print.

Davies, Roger J. and, Osamu Ikeno. *The Japanese Mind: Understanding Contemporary Japanese Culture*. North Clarendon: Tuttle Publishing, 2005. Print.

de Mooij, Marieke. *Global Marketing and Advertising*. Thousand Oaks: Sage Publications, Inc., 2014. Print.

Hyun, Jane. *Breaking the Bamboo Ceiling: Career Strategies for Asians*. New York: HarperBusiness, 2005. Print.

Institute of International Education. *Open Doors Report*. New York: November, 2013. Print.

Kim, Myung Oak and Sam Jaffe. *The New Korea: An Inside Look at South Korea's Economic Rise*. New York: Amacom, 2010. Print.

Mason, Colin. *A Short History of Asia*. 2nd ed. New York: Palgrave Macmillan, 2005. Print.

Morton, W. Scott, Charlton M. Lewis and Charlton Lewis. *China: Its History and Culture*. 4th ed. New York: McGraw Hill, 2004. Print.

Mueller, Barbara. *Dynamics of International Advertising*. New York: Peter Lang, 2011. Print.

Norbury, Paul. *Japan - Culture Smart!: The Essential Guide to Customs & Culture*. Revised. London: Kuperard, 2011. Print.

Samovar, Larry A. and Richard E. Porter. *Communication between Cultures*. Belmont: Wadsworth Publishing Company, 1991. Print.

Wächter, Arnd, Dawn Pysarchik, Brett Berquist, and Peter Briggs. *The Dialogue*. Crossing Borders Education and Michigan State University, 2013. http://www.cb-films.org/thedialogue

Wenzhong, Hu, Cornelius N. Grove and Zhuang Enping. *Encountering the Chinese: A Modern Country, An Ancient Culture*. 3rd ed. Boston: Intercultural Press, 2010. Print.

Wilkinson, Sook and Victor Jew, eds. *Asian Americans in Michigan*. Detroit: Wayne State University Press, 2015. Print.

Wu, Frank. *Yellow: Race in America Beyond Black and White*, reprint. New York: Basic Books, 2003. Print.

Zia, Helen. *Asian American Dreams: The Emergence of an American People*. New York: Farrar, Straus and Giroux, 2001. Print.

Also in This Series

100 Questions and Answers About Americans
100 Questions and Answers About Arab Americans
100 Questions and Answers About Hispanics and Latinos
100 Questions and Answers About Indian Americans
100 Questions, 500 Nations: A Guide to Native America

For copies

Copies of this guide in paperback or ebook formats may be ordered from Amazon. For a volume discount on copies or a special edition customized and braded for your university or organization, contact David Crumm Media, LLC at info@ DavidCrummMedia.com.

For more information and further discussion visit: news. jrn.msu.edu/culturalcompetence

If you enjoyed this book, you may also enjoy

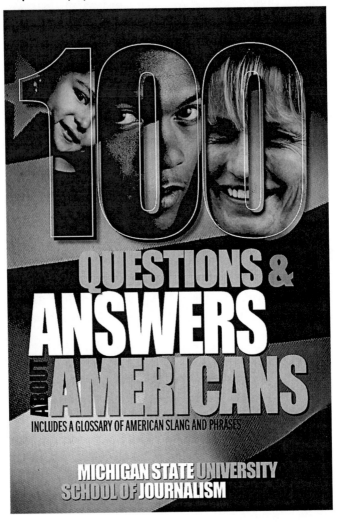

100

QUESTIONS &
ANSWERS
ABOUT AMERICANS

INCLUDES A GLOSSARY OF AMERICAN SLANG AND PHRASES

MICHIGAN STATE UNIVERSITY
SCHOOL OF JOURNALISM

This questions and answers guide from the Michigan
State University School of Journalism provides 100
answers to basic questions about Americans.

http://news.jrn.msu.edu/culturalcompetence/

ISBN: 978-1-939880-20-8

If you enjoyed this book, you may also enjoy

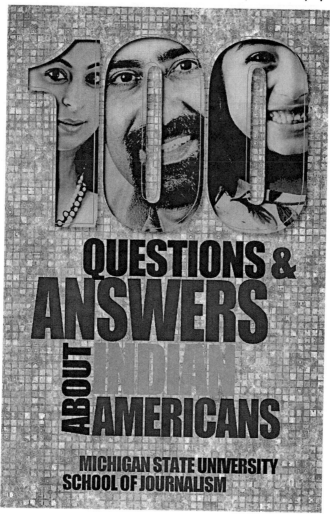

This questions and answers guide from the Michigan State University School of Journalism provides 100 answers to basic questions about Indian Americans.

http://news.jrn.msu.edu/culturalcompetence/

ISBN: 978-1-939880-00-0

If you enjoyed this book, you may also enjoy

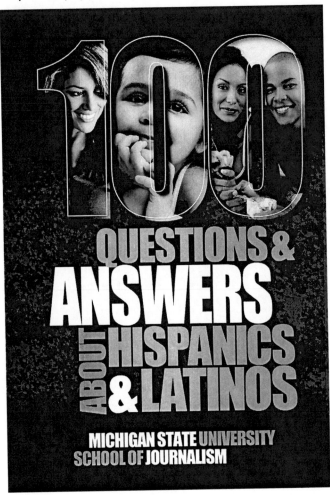

This questions and answers guide from the Michigan State University School of Journalism provides 100 answers to basic questions about Hispanics and Latinos.

http://news.jrn.msu.edu/culturalcompetence/

ISBN: 978-1-939880-44-4

If you enjoyed this book, you may also enjoy

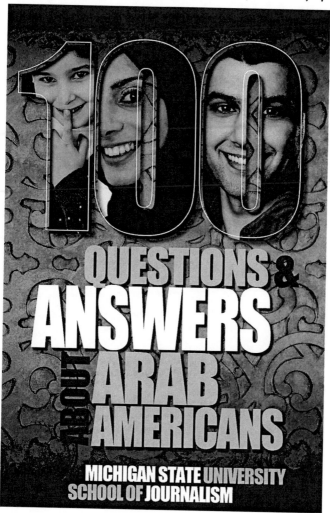

This questions and answers guide from the Michigan State University School of Journalism provides 100 answers to basic questions about Arab Americans.

http://news.jrn.msu.edu/culturalcompetence/

978-1-939880-56-7

CPSIA information can be obtained at www.ICGtesting.com
Printed in the USA
BVOW02s0022010416

442574BV00001B/7/P